Gathering Wisdom

A Devotional Walk through the Books of the Bible

Peggy Musgrove

Table of Contents

Dedication

To my three grandchildren,
Colin, Christopher, and **Grace,**
and to the generations to come,
with the sincere desire that they have lifelong
communication with God
through their knowlege of His Word.

Acknowledgements

This book would not have been completed without the help
of my daughters, **Darla** and **Diane**,
and their husbands, **Rick Knoth** and **David Awbrey**.
All are professionals in the field of publication.
My granddaughter **Grace Awbrey** assisted with entering copy.

My late husband **Derald Musgrove**, who always had a camera with him
to preserve the beauty of nature, took all the photographs.

So this book is a family project.

v

Introduction

This book is the product of a liftetime of Bible study. The content was shared first in weekly format on Facebook as "Monday Meditations." My decision to publish this book was to preserve the notes for future reference, particularly for my family.

The theme of the articles is "Communicating with God." God speaks to us through His Word; we speak to Him in prayer.

Communication occurs while walking through the Scriptures, one book at a time, gathering wisdom as we would gather flowers while walking through a garden.

Hence the title *Gathering Wisdom* and the subtitle *A Devotional Walk through the Books of the Bible* describe the experience of this book. The photographs create a virtual garden to remind us of the pleasure of a garden walk.

Reading through the Bible annually, a practice I learned from my mother, is my most valuable habit. The Scriptures relate to every area of life.

As I approach the end of my days on earth, I often think about what I will leave to my family. My greatest desire is that they follow Jesus. Bible knowledge is essential to achieving that goal.

I hope many people will take this journey with me, by personalizing the concepts and engaging their own communication with God, gathering wisdom from His Word.

Peggy Musgrove

In the beginning

God...

Genesis 1:1

The Book of Beginnings

*G*enesis is called the Book of Beginnings, because of its opening phrase: "In the beginning God . . . ."

The Bible opens by acknowledging God's existence. The writer does not attempt to prove His being; He simply "is." A mathematician might call His presence the "given," an assumption we accept as presented.

The first three chapters present other beginnings. We see the beginning of the heavens and earth, the animal kingdom, and the human race. We also see the beginning of sin.

God communicated directly with Adam and Eve and put them in charge of His creation (1:28–29). But they disobeyed Him, and sin entered the world (3:6). In her conversation with the serpent, Eve misquotes what God had commanded. She sought for pleasure and wisdom from another source, rather than communicating with God (3:6). Genesis 3:15 gives the first hint of God's salvation plan when He said someone would "crush" the serpent's head.

The first reference to prayer comes in the next chapter: "At that time people began to call on the name of the LORD" (4:26). The word *prayer* isn't mentioned, but this simple phrase defines what prayer is—calling on the name of the Lord.

Humanity sensed a need to restore the communication with God that was lost when sin entered the Garden of Eden. Communication was renewed by simply calling to God in prayer.

Prayer: Lord, we join the ancients and call on Your name today. We live in a sinful world, and we need Your forgiveness.

Moses built an altar and called it
the Lord is my Banner.
Exodus 17:15

A Place to Worship

When people began communicating with God, their lives became purposeful. Noah heard God's voice asking him to build an ark. It seemed like a formidable task, but Noah's obedience saved his family during a flood.

Abraham believed God when He said Abraham's descendants would become a nation. This prophecy stretched his faith because Abraham was childless, but in God's time Isaac, the son of promise, was born.

Isaac's son Jacob, later called Israel, had 12 sons. When life got tough, they went to Egypt. When life got tough again, their descendants wanted to go home to Canaan. Again, God spoke to a man, Moses, to do a specific work. Moses needed wisdom to lead the family that became a nation.

What was the source of Moses' wisdom? He communicated with God! When Moses took time to turn aside from his daily duty, he heard God's voice call him to an amazing journey.

Once, after a busy day of battle, "Moses built an altar" (17:15). This phrase describes Moses' habit of finding a place to talk with God as he led the nation of Israel.

When the ancients—from Noah, to Abraham, to Moses—gave God time and place, He revealed His purpose for their lives.

Prayer: Lord, help me find places to call upon Your name—a place in my time, a place in my thoughts, and a place in my heart. I want to know Your purpose for my life.

The Lord *bless you*
and *keep you;*
the Lord make his face
shine on you and be
gracious to you;
the Lord turn his face
toward you
and give you *peace.*

Numbers 6:24-26

Guide for Prayer

*E*gyptian law no longer governed the Children of Israel after they crossed the Red Sea. To guide this vast group of people, God gave Moses a set of laws specifically for them.

Exodus contains the Ten Commandments, the best known of all the Old Testament laws. Leviticus and Numbers contain other ceremonial laws and their enforcement. Within the regulations, God included instructions for praying.

So far we have not seen many prayers recorded word-for-word. We only read that people prayed. In the Book of Numbers, God gives an actual prayer to Aaron:

> The LORD bless you and keep you;
> The LORD make his face shine on you
>   and be gracious to you;
> The LORD turn his face toward you
>   and give you peace. (Numbers 6:24-26)

Many churches use this prayer for formal dismissal. Studying it gives guidelines for personal praying. The LORD is referred to three times. He is the God who blesses and protects. His face shows acceptance and love. He bestows grace and peace. In summary, God protects, provides, and gives peace. Knowing I am cared for by that kind of God blesses me.

The priests prayed this prayer over Israel. You can make it your personal prayer by inserting the word *me* for each *you*. The concepts can be enlarged in your own words.

Prayer: *Lord, help us to pray effectively. We need Your protection, Your provision, and Your peace.*

Love the Lord your God
with all your *heart* and
with all your *soul* and
with all your *strength.*

Deuteronomy 6:5

"Get" What God Says

*W*hen your parents said something twice, did you listen? They told you twice so you would "get" what they said.

Moses reviews much of the Law in Deuteronomy so Israel will "get" what God said. Moses' farewell address to the nation is included in this book.

Though Deuteronomy is a part of the Law, the love of God is the emphasis of the book.

> Love the LORD your God with all your heart and with all your soul and with all your strength. (6:5)

Jesus quoted this verse in Matthew 22:36–40, saying it was the greatest commandment.

Moses made the right way of living very plain. He said, "Seek the LORD your God, you will find him if you seek him with all your heart and with all your soul" (4:29).

We know that Israel did not listen or obey. The key word in this sentence is the little word IF.

God is concerned not only with laws but also with relationships. God waits for us. He does not play hide-and-seek with us, but our sins, and sometimes our busy lives, get in the way.

We can know His heart of love, IF we look for Him with all our heart! And IF our heart is elsewhere, for whatever reason, we walk on alone.

Prayer: *Lord, in simplicity we come to You with all our heart. We desire Your presence so our lives will please You.*

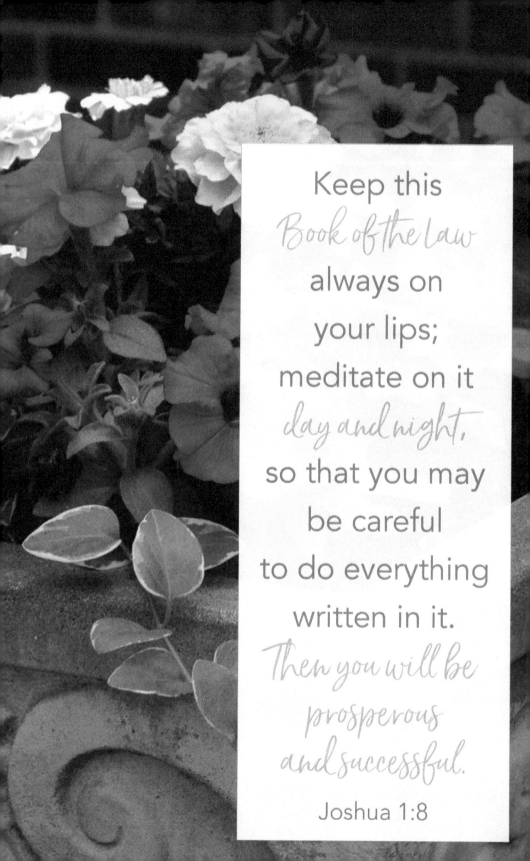

Keep this
Book of the law
always on
your lips;
meditate on it
day and night,
so that you may
be careful
to do everything
written in it.
Then you will be
prosperous
and successful.

Joshua 1:8

Meditate Day and Night

*C*ommunicating with God is a two-way conversation. We talk to Him in prayer; He speaks to us through His Word where we find wisdom.

In his final words, Moses reminded Joshua, who followed him as Israel's leader, of the importance of God's Word:

> Keep this Book of the Law always on your lips; meditate on it day and night, so that you may be careful to do everything written in it. Then you will be prosperous and successful. (1:8)

Moses knew Joshua would face difficult situations. What would be the source of Joshua's strength? Meditating on God's Word.

Since Jesus came, we no longer keep Old Testament rituals. Christ was the fulfillment of the ceremonial Law. But the moral principles remain the same—summed up briefly by Jesus as loving God and loving others as ourselves.

How do we face everyday challenges and live a life of love? The same way Joshua did—knowing God's Word and living by it.

When the Bible speaks of knowing God's Word, it often infers experiential knowledge. Knowing God's Word is not just collecting information as we do in studying math or history.

We know God's Word is true because we have experienced its effect in our lives. His Word lives in our minds and hearts.

Prayer: Lord, like Joshua, we need courage to face our daily challenges. Teach us from Your Word; help us make it a part of our lives. May we share Your love everywhere.

Choose for yourselves this day
whom you will serve . . . .
But as for me
and my household,
we will serve the Lord.

Joshua 24:15

Rules for Universal Living

*R*emember what happened in school when the teacher left the classroom? Chaos erupted! That kind of disorder pervaded Israel in Judges when there was no national authority:

> In those days, Israel had no king;
> everyone did as they saw fit. (17:6)

Moses and Joshua, leaders of the past, are now dead. Judges are ruling in some areas, but no national leadership existed. People live by their own rules.

Who has authority to make rules? Parents make rules for children. Governments make rules for citizens. Are there universal rules everyone should follow? Bible believers say "yes."

The Bible gives guidance for citizens of the universe. God's authority comes from His creative power shown in Genesis. As Creator, He owns the universe with the right to make rules.

The Old Testament gives many rules for universal living. Previously, we mentioned that Jesus summarized these rules as "Love God and love your neighbor as yourselves."

When we recognize God as our Creator, we acknowledge His Word has authority over our lives. We would do well to remember Joshua's wise words in his final charge to Israel:

> Choose for yourselves this day whom you will serve. . . .
> But as for me and my household, we will serve the LORD.
> (Joshua 24:15)

Prayer: Lord, today we choose to serve You and follow Your rules. We want our lives to reflect love, for You, for our neighbors, and for ourselves.

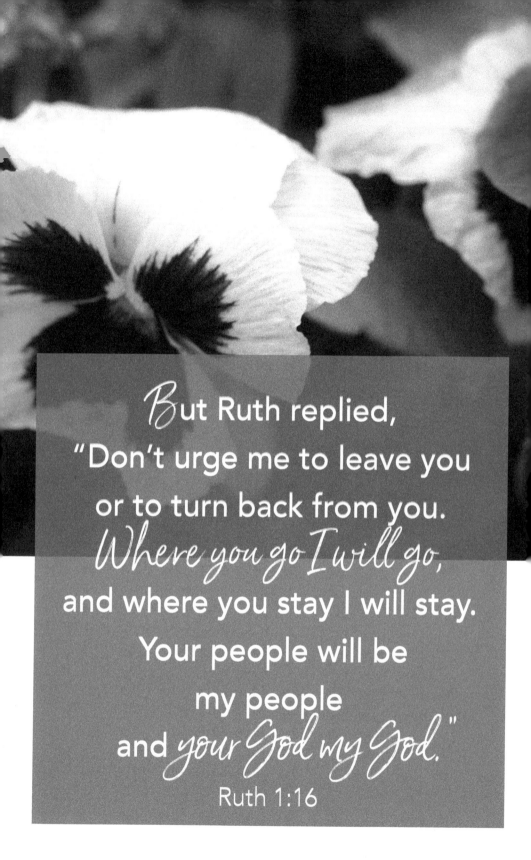

But Ruth replied, "Don't urge me to leave you or to turn back from you. *Where you go I will go,* and where you stay I will stay. Your people will be my people and *your God my God.*"

Ruth 1:16

Ruth

A Most Important Choice

A love story interrupts Israel's historical account. The narration changes focus from Israel's history to one family's problems. In the Book of Ruth, we see how God sovereignly leads, even in individual, difficult situations.

Because of a great famine, Elimelek, a resident of Bethlehem, takes his wife, Naomi, and two sons to Moab. The sons marry Moabite women; then both of them and their father die, leaving three widows.

The love story begins when Naomi decides to return home and tells her daughters-in-law to return to their parents. But Ruth reacts:

> "Don't urge me to leave you . . . . Where you go, I will go . . . . Your people will be my people, and your God, my God." (1:16)

The Bible does not say much about Naomi's spiritual life, but something about her impresses Ruth. Consequently, she is willing to leave her family to be with Naomi and Naomi's God.

Ruth's choice to go with Naomi affected her personally, socially, and spiritually. Her most important choice was accepting God—the most important choice anyone can make.

In the last chapter, we read that Ruth became the great-grandmother of King David, the ancestor of Jesus. If we choose to follow Jesus, our last chapter will be that we spend eternity with Him.

Personal and social choices affect us in this life, but spiritual choices affect us for eternity.

Prayer: Lord, help us make right choices today—for both time and eternity!

Go in peace,
and may the God of Israel
grant you what you have
asked of him.

1 Samuel 1:17

Praying for Peace

*A*woman whose prayers influenced a nation appears in the first chapter of this historical narrative of Israel. At that time, having children gave a woman status and security. Hannah was childless.

Hannah prayed earnestly, and God gave her a son who became a prominent national figure—a transitional leader who anointed the first two kings of Israel. We learn much from Hannah's prayer in 1 Samuel 1:10-17. Read it—and note these things:

She continued praying in spite of an aching heart.

> Hannah's childlessness caused her much sorrow, but she did not sink into self-pity. In her brokenness, she wept before the Lord. (1:10)

She continued praying in spite of misunderstanding.

> Hannah shared her heart in silent communication with the Lord. The priest assumed she was drunk because of her brokenness (1:13).

She continued praying until she had peace.

> When the priest finally recognized her need, he gave her his blessing (1:17). First Samuel 1:18 concludes, "Her countenance was no more sad." Her circumstance had not yet changed, but her countenance had.

Samuel, the son for whom Hannah prayed, became the transitional leader of Israel. He anointed the nation's first two kings, Saul and David. 1 and 2 Samuel carry the stories of those two dynasties.

Prayer: Lord, help us communicate with You as Hannah did. Heal our aching, hurting hearts, and give us peace as only You can give.

$\mathcal{G}$ive your servant a
discerning heart
to govern your people and to
distinguish between
right and wrong.

1 Kings 3:9

Making Wise Choices

*I*f God said to you, "Ask whatever you want me to give you," what would you say? This happened to Solomon after he was anointed as king of Israel.

We are told that "Solomon showed his love for the LORD by walking according to the instructions given him by his father" (1 Kings 3:3).

At this point, Solomon prayed a model prayer:

- He acknowledged God's greatness,
- He thanked God for His kindness,
- He recognized his own weakness, and
- He requested wisdom from God (1 Kings 3:6-9).

God honored his request for wisdom, and He added riches and honor. Under Solomon, Israel reached its greatest heights as a nation.

But that is not the end of the story. Solomon was a smart man who made foolish choices. His wise mind gave way to his wandering heart.

Other types of love diluted his love for God:

> King Solomon, however, loved many foreign women . . . . As Solomon grew old, his wives turned his heart away after other gods, and his heart was not fully devoted to the LORD his God. (1 Kings 11:1, 4)

These alliances brought Solomon's downfall, and the entire nation crumbled as a result of his choices.

Prayer: *Lord, purify our hearts from alliances that keep us from loving You supremely. May our lifestyle reflect our total love for You.*

If my people,
who are called
by my name,
will humble
themselves
and pray
and seek
my face and
turn from
their wicked ways,
then I will hear
from heaven, and
I will
forgive their sin
and will
heal their land.

2 Chronicles 7:14

Praying for Ourselves and Others

*C*ommunication with God includes praying for ourselves and others. In the Chronicles, we see examples of both types of prayer.

The prayer of Jabez is well-known:

> Jabez cried out to the God of Israel, "Oh, that you would bless me and enlarge my territory. Let your hand be with me, and keep me from harm." (1 Chronicles 4:10)

Jabez prayed for himself that he would have God's blessing, His provision, and His protection. This prayer is legitimate, but our prayers must go beyond ourselves. Christians are intended to live in community.

Another well-known verse in the Chronicles tells us how to pray with others:

> If my people, who are called by my name, will humble themselves and pray and seek my face and turn from their wicked ways, then I will hear from heaven, and I will forgive their sin and will heal their land. (2 Chronicles 7:14)

In this prayer we:

- Identify with the people of God.
- Recognize our collective dependence on God.
- Consecrate our lives to God.
- Trust Him for our wellbeing as a nation.

Prayer: Lord, like Jabez, we pray for our personal needs, but we also pray that You will "enlarge our territory" so we will think of the needs of others.

Ezra had devoted
himself to the
study and observance
of the Law of the LORD,
and to teaching
its decrees and laws
in Israel.

Ezra 7:10

Building Our Life on His Word

Communication with God takes as many forms as conversation with a good friend. The Book of Ezra illustrates this variety very clearly.

Historically, we have read past the eras when kings ruled Israel and later when the nation was in captivity. Ezra lived during the time that Israel was about to be restored to its homeland. Ezra 7:10 gives us the key to the book:

> Ezra had devoted himself to the study and observance of the law of the LORD, and to teaching its decrees and laws in Israel.

This wise decision involved Ezra's whole being. Emotionally, he longed for God's Word; intellectually, he studied it. Willfully, he "devoted himself" (or "set his heart," KJV) not only to study it, but also to live by it and teach it to others.

From this foundational knowledge of God's Word, Ezra's prayer life took many forms.

- He engaged in formal worship (3:3-5).
- He sang praise to the Lord when he saw the restoration of the temple (3:10-11).
- He joyfully celebrated Jewish holidays given in their law (6:22).
- He prayed for himself, his friends, and their children (8:21).
- He wept and prayed for the sins of his fellow Israelites (10:1).

Prayer: *Lord, help us to build our lives on Your Word. May our prayers include sincere worship as we trust You for personal needs and intercede for the needs of others.*

The king said to me,
"What is it you want?"
Then *I prayed*
to the God of heaven,
and *I answered* the king.

Nehemiah 2:4-5

Spontaneous Prayer

*H*ave you ever uttered a "quick" prayer—maybe when a car swerved at you in traffic? Nehemiah introduces that kind of prayer.

Nehemiah lived in Babylon before Israel was restored to its homeland. Like Ezra, Nehemiah talked with God about his beloved nation.

The first chapter pictures Nehemiah sorrowfully praying long days for his people. The second chapter introduces the spontaneous prayer.

A delegation returned from the homeland, bringing a bad report. The heartbroken Nehemiah could not spend days in prayer because he was employed by the king.

Culturally, servants were to be cheerful in the king's presence. So when the king asked Nehemiah why he was sad, Nehemiah was frightened. He told the king about his concern for his people, and surprisingly, he got a favorable response.

Nehemiah prayed the "quick" prayer in the split-second between the king's question and Nehemiah's answer:

> Then I prayed to the God of heaven, and I answered the king. (Nehemiah 2:4-5)

Nehemiah's prayer could not have been verbal or lengthy. It was like the silent, unverbalized prayers we cannot utter.

The beauty of regular communication with God is that when tough situations arise, we can instinctively cry out to Him, knowing He will hear us.

Prayer: Lord, I want You to hear my voice regularly, so You'll recognize me when I'm desperate.

And who knows
but that you have come
to your royal position
*for such a time
as this?*

Esther 4:14

A Timely Prayer

*I*s prayer alone enough? When do we "give feet" to our prayers? The Book of Esther helps answer these questions.

Esther is an unusual book in that prayer, worship, and the name of God are not mentioned. Yet we see God moving on behalf of His people when they do what they can for themselves.

Esther, an orphan who became queen, is in the unique position of being the only person who can act to save her nation. Mordecai, her cousin and caregiver, suggests that this moment is the purpose for which she became queen. He says,

> "And who knows but that you have come to your royal position for such a time as this?" (4:14).

Before Queen Esther acts, she calls for a fast—the only spiritual activity mentioned in the book. Culturally, at that time, a fast would include prayer.

Esther's courageous response to go against protocol meant putting her life on the line. Her words are well known:

> "And if I perish, I perish" (4:16).

The rest is history. She did what she could, and she saved her nation.

Our position may not be as prominent as that of a queen, so our actions are not as far-reaching. But our unique position includes influence that only we can have.

Prayer: Lord, help us understand Your unique purpose for our lives. Help us know when to pray and when to "give feet" to our prayers.

I know that
my redeemer lives,
and that in the end
he will stand
on the earth.

My Redeemer Lives

Would you deny your faith in God if you had a series of catastrophes? What if your friends claimed your sin caused your misfortunates or your spouse harangued you for continuing to believe that God loves you? Those were Job's dilemmas, and he kept his faith.

We have finished the sections of Law and History. Job's story is in the book by his name, the first of five poetic books we explore next.

The Book of Job is a Jewish narrative poem. The opening and closing chapters tell of Job's problems and restoration. In between, his friends accuse him of causing his own troubles.

In the end, God rebukes the friends and talks with Job. Consequently, Job confesses his human weakness and failure to trust.

One verse gives insight into Job's character, helping us understand how he remained faithful even when his wife wanted him to "curse God and die." Job had an unfaltering belief in God:

> I know that my redeemer lives, and that in the end he will stand on the earth. (Job 19:25)

We see the process of spiritual growth in Job. He goes through questioning and despair before he has a personal encounter with God. His response is repentance and recognition of his weakness. Job does not always understand, but he always believes.

Prayer: Lord, help us to trust Your heart of love, even when we cannot see Your hand at work.

Every morning
you'll hear me
at it again.
Every morning
I lay out the pieces
of my life on
your altar and
watch for fire
to descend.

Psalm 5:3, MSG

God Is Sovereign

*I*s prayer always pretty? Can we talk about the ugly things in our life to God? Can we tell God our real thoughts and feelings? The psalmists did.

The psalms come from many writers and times. They span more than a thousand years, yet they contain themes consistent with other Scriptures.

God is sovereign in the Book of Psalms. We see His wisdom, power, and presence. We see Him as the caring Creator. We get glimpses of Christ's future Kingdom and our eternal home.

We quote some psalms because of their beauty. Psalm 23 talks about peaceful green pastures and still waters. Other psalms, such as Psalm 109, shock us with expressions of raw emotions—anger, fear, and despair.

As we read the Psalms, we discover the psalmists expressing their deepest thoughts to God. This is authenticity in praying—no pretense, just laying everything before God.

We know God heard the psalmists' prayers. Let's join with King David who committed in Psalm 5 to pray every morning. I like Eugene H. Peterson's paraphrase in *The Message:*

> Every morning you'll hear me at it again. Every morning I lay out the pieces of my life on your altar and watch for fire to descend. (5:3)

Prayer: *Lord, we don't offer ritual sacrifices as David did, but we do ask for Your fire to consume everything wrong in our lives and to consecrate what is right.*

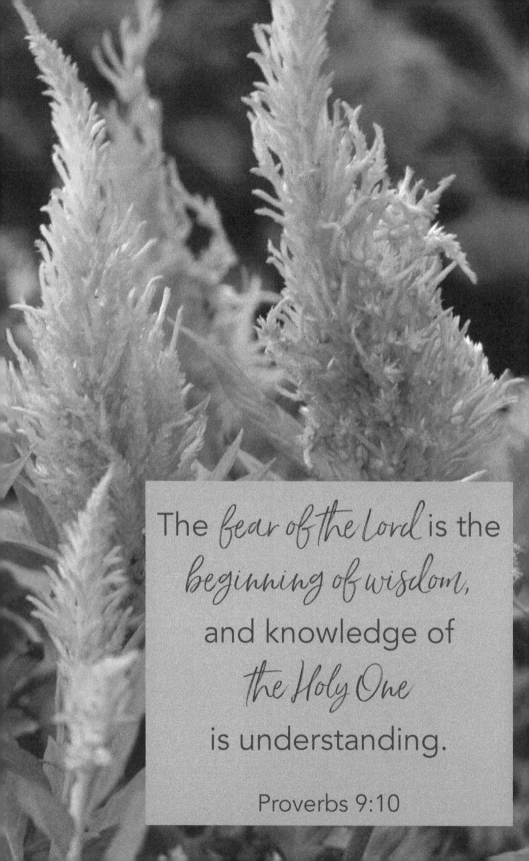

The *fear of the Lord* is the *beginning of wisdom,* and knowledge of *the Holy One* is understanding.

Proverbs 9:10

Practical Wisdom

*D*id your parents have short, pithy reminders they repeated as you went out the door? My mother had many, which I quoted so often to my daughters they labeled them "Hazel's Happy Household Hints!"

The Book of Proverbs contains those kinds of sayings. Most are credited to Solomon, but some come from others. They include experiential wisdom passed down through the generations.

The psalms primarily deal with our relationship to God and our spiritual wellbeing. The proverbs deal more with our relationship to people. Our relationship with God is revealed in our relationship with others.

One of the purposes of the Book of Proverbs is to give knowledge to the young. Reading one of the 31 chapters each day each month is a great way to absorb this practical wisdom.

The poetic form most used is the two-line couplet. The second line extends or explains the first line or sometimes contrasts with it. The lines do not rhyme like the poetry that may be more familiar to us.

The theme of the Book of Proverbs is summarized in the ninth chapter:

> The fear of the Lord is the beginning of wisdom, and knowledge of the Holy One is understanding. (9:10)

Prayer: Lord, You gave us much practical wisdom in the Book of Proverbs; help us to wisely follow Your Word and not foolishly ignore it.

Remember your *Creator* in the days of your youth . . .

Ecclesiastes 12:1

What Matters?

What really matters? Every day someone gives a different answer. This question is not only a 21st century one; Solomon asked it many centuries before Christ.

Ecclesiastes and the Song of Songs are usually attributed to Solomon, the richest and wisest of Israel's kings. When I read these books, I imagine Solomon as an old king sitting at the palace gate with his lyre beside him. Daily, he ponders the question, "What matters?"

Ecclesiastes records Solomon's thoughts about pleasure, riches, and success. He had it all—more than any other human being in his time. His conclusion? None of it matters. Everything this world offers is worthless, as empty as a punctured balloon.

The old king picks up his lyre to sing. One of his thousand songs is recorded as the Song of Songs. He sings about the elusiveness of human love, reflecting on the endurance of love for God.

At the end of life, what matters to the old king? His answer: nothing matters but a relationship with God. His wise advice to us:

> Remember your Creator in the days of your youth, before the days of trouble come and the years approach when you will say, "I find no pleasure in them." (Ecclesiastes 12:1)

Prayer: Lord, help us focus on our relationship with You, whatever our age, so we can live the rest of our life without regrets.

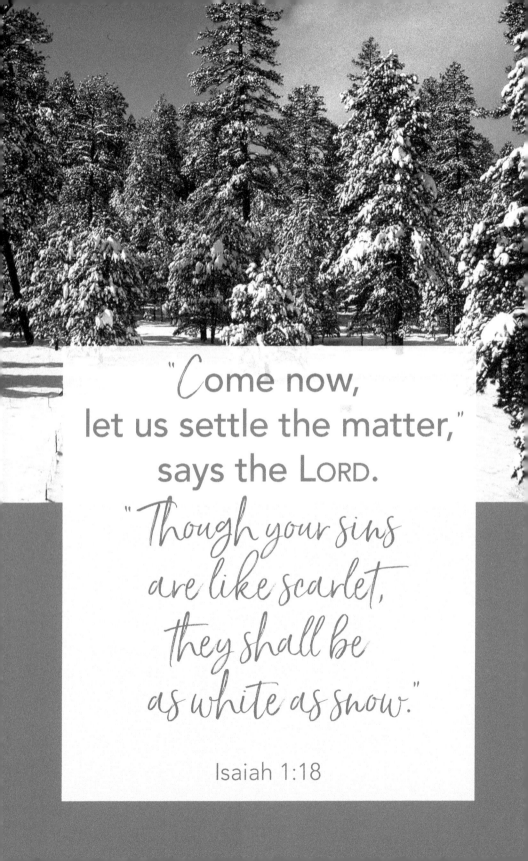

"Come now,
let us settle the matter,"
says the LORD.
"Though your sins
are like scarlet,
they shall be
as white as snow."

Isaiah 1:18

Assured of His Presence

*W*hat is a prophet? Classic cartoons picture a prophet as a bearded man holding a shepherd's staff and a sign saying, "The end is near."

As we walk through the Bible, we meet real prophets, not cartoon characters. Some were priests; others were advisors to kings. A few might fit the cartoon image, but all were dynamic representatives for God.

The longer prophetic books of the Bible are designated as Major Prophets. Isaiah, the author of the first prophetic book, writes on many themes, about his own time and the future.

Some prophecies are of the coming Messiah:

> For unto us a child is born. (9:6)

> He was pierced for our transgressions. (53:5)

Others give a call to repentance:

> "Come now, let us settle the matter," says the Lord. "Though your sins are like scarlet, they shall be as white as snow." (1:18)

Isaiah repeatedly assures people of God's presence. When I left home for college almost 70 years ago, I took one assuring verse as God speaking directly to me:

> Do not fear, for I am with you; do not be dismayed, for I am your God. I will strengthen you and help you; I will uphold you with my righteous right hand. (41:10)

He has always been with me. The God of the Bible still speaks to us today through His Word.

Prayer: Lord, You communicate with us through Your Word. Help us respond by living by what You have said.

Call to me
and I will
answer you
and tell you
great and
unsearchable
things you
do not know.

Jeremiah 33:3

Assured of His Faithfulness

Jeremiah sort of fits the image of the cartoon prophet. Isaiah counseled kings before Jeremiah was born. By contrast, Jeremiah the priest was a loner from a small village, and the villagers rejected him.

Isaiah talked about hope and the Messiah; Jeremiah warned of judgment and the fall of his nation. Jeremiah suffered greatly for his prophecies, even though many came true in his lifetime. Through his suffering, he learned about the faithfulness of God.

While Jeremiah was in prison, God spoke these words to him:

> Call to me and I will answer you and tell you great and unsearchable things you do not know. (Jeremiah 33:3)

Even in that dark time, God communicated with Jeremiah.

The Book of Lamentations is a collection of Jeremiah's poems revealing his heart in those lonely hours. In the Hebrew language, the poems are skillfully arranged in acrostic form. Even in English, however, their lofty message is not obscured:

> Yet this I call to mind and therefore I have hope:

> Because of the LORD's great love we are not consumed, for his compassions never fail.

> They are new every morning; great is your faithfulness. (Lamentations 3:21-23)

From Jeremiah's experiences, we know we can communicate with God in hours of great suffering, and He will faithfully communicate with us.

Prayer: Lord, help us to look beyond our circumstances to see Your loving kindness that is new every morning, just as Jeremiah said.

Then you will know that

I am the Lord,

when I bring you into
the land of Israel,
the land I had sworn to
give to your ancestors.

Ezekiel 20:42

God Reveals Himself

*H*ow do we know there is a God? Ezekiel deals with that question. More than 70 times Ezekiel quotes God as saying something will happen, followed by the phrase, "then you will know that I am the LORD" (11:10).

God revealed himself at the beginning in nature. The Psalmist affirmed this connection: "The heavens declare the glory of God" (Psalm 19:1).

God reveals himself in His Word. He gave the Law to Moses, and discloses His nature in biblical writings.

God reveals himself by His Spirit. The Old and New Testaments relate many personal encounters with God.

Obedient people respond to these positive revelations and live in communication with God. Ezekiel tells of not-so-positive things that happen to the disobedient.

Ezekiel prophesies that because of Israel's disobedience, God will reveal himself in judgment. Desolation will come to them.

But Ezekiel also foretells Israel's final restoration. In spite of their waywardness, ultimately God's mercy will be extended:

> Then you will know that I am the LORD, when I bring you into the land of Israel, the land I had sworn with uplifted hand to give to your ancestors. (20:42)

This restoration happened after 70 years of captivity in that era. It happened again in the 20th century when Jews returned to Israel after the Holocaust of World War II. Israel is still a nation today.

Prayer: Lord, help us respond positively to Your Word and your Spirit, so You do not have to judge us.

Three times a day he got down on his knees and prayed, giving thanks to his God, just as he had done before.

Daniel 6:10-11

A Consistent Prayer Life

Character is revealed by the choices we make when we are alone.

Daniel's character emerged shortly after he became a prisoner in Babylon. When non-kosher food was set before him, he opted not to eat it. He didn't pray about it; he knew the right thing to do.

Daniel's character showed again when his life was threatened because no one could interpret the king's dream. When Daniel heard this, he responded, "with wisdom and tact" (2:14). He asked his friends to join him to "plead for mercy from the God of heaven" (2:18). God revealed the dream to Daniel, and his life was spared, along with many others.

The greatest test of character came much later when a new king passed a law against praying to God. However, that did not stop Daniel.

> Three times a day he got down on his knees and prayed, giving thanks to his God, just as he had done before. (6:10-11)

You probably know what happened. He ended up in the lion's den, but God protected him from harm.

Daniel lived nearly 70 years in a foreign land, serving four kings. He maintained his godly character and consistent prayer life. He gave distinct prophecies of gentile kingdoms and end-time events.

Prayer: Lord, help us to do the right thing when the choice is obvious. Help us depend on You in situations beyond our control.

For I desire mercy,
not sacrifice, and
acknowledgment of God
rather than burnt offerings.
Hosea 6:6

The Compassionate Heart of God

*D*o you ever wonder what God looks like? Though we don't see His face, prophets such as Hosea help us see His heart.

Hosea is the first of the Minor Prophets—those who wrote shorter books. He prophesied for 38 years without seeing many results.

Hosea's marriage to Gomer, an adulterous woman, is an allegory of God's love for an unfaithful nation. Hosea's willingness to forgive Gomer reflects the compassionate heart of God.

Hosea records this message from God that reveals His heart:

> For I desire mercy and not sacrifice, and acknowledgement of God rather than burnt offerings. (6:6)

God longs for His people to know He is more interested in relationship than in rituals. The practices of religion mean nothing to Him if they do not come from a loving heart.

When Gomer's lovers plot to sell her into slavery, Hosea buys her and takes her to his home again. His action illustrates God's forgiveness to rebellious Israel (and to us).

Hosea closes his writings with solemn words:

> The ways of the LORD are right; the righteous walk in them, but the rebellious stumble in them. (14:9)

Prayer: Lord, help us understand Hosea's message—that You want us to serve You out of love. Please, keep our feet from straying.

I will
pour out my Spirit
on all people.

Joel 2:28

Call for Repentance and Prayer

*C*artoonists could point to Joel as their model. An unidentified prophet from an unknown place, Joel appears announcing judgment.

Unlike the cartoon prophet, Joel includes a message of hope. The apostle Peter affirms Joel's prophecy by quoting him on the Day of Pentecost.

Joel uses the phrase "Blow the trumpet in Zion" (2:1) to introduce his prophecies. A trumpet blast was the "instant messaging" signal of his day.

The first trumpet blast warns of coming judgment:

> A day of darkness and gloom, a day of clouds and blackness. (2:2)

This message includes God's perennial call to repentance:

> Return to the Lord your God, for He is gracious and compassionate, slow to anger and abounding in love. (2:13)

The second trumpet blast is a call to prayer because enemies are ridiculing the nation. The call is so urgent that weddings are to be canceled. The people respond and hear God's promise of restoration.

Included in that promise is the prophecy of the coming of the Holy Spirit:

> I will pour out my Spirit on all people. (2:28)

Peter acknowledges this prophecy hundreds of years later when the Holy Spirit moves on early believers at the beginning of the Church Age (Acts 2:18). The Holy Spirit still empowers the Church today.

Prayer: Lord, help us feel the urgency Joel felt when he issued that call to prayer. We have an urgent need for the power of Your Spirit today.

Seek good,

not evil, that you may live. *Then the Lord Almighty will be with you.*

Amos 5:14

Worship from a Clean Heart

*A*mos probably would be wearing cowboy boots and a big hat if he appeared today. He denied being a prophet; he was "one of the shepherds of Tekoa," (like a cowboy only he herded sheep).

Israel had been divided since Rehoboam's reign. The northern kingdom was still called Israel. Amos was from the southern kingdom of Judah.

When Amos appeared to prophesy in the northern kingdom, he was an outsider. He was accepted because he prophesied the destruction of Israel's enemies. Cheers and loud "amens" probably filled the town square when he spoke.

But then he started naming Israel's sins. His prophecies probably came at different times, but they are recorded together in one book.

Amos, emphasizing the sovereignty of God, called for repentance and right living:

> Seek good, not evil, that you may live.
> Then the LORD God Almighty will be with you. (5:14)

The Children of Israel prided themselves on keeping the Law. But Amos shocked them by saying God did not want their ritualistic worship.

When they asked what God did want, Amos answered:

> But let justice roll on like a river,
> righteousness like a never-failing stream! (5:24)

Like other prophets, Amos emphasized that God wants worship from a clean heart, accompanied by right actions. He wants the same today.

Prayer: *Lord, help us learn from what Amos said, and live in right relationship with You and those around us.*

From inside the fish *Jonah prayed to the Lord his God.* He said: "In my distress I called to the LORD, and he answered me."

Jonah 2:1-2

A Merciful God

God is not a local deity; He is Sovereign over the entire world. Obadiah and Jonah help us see Him this way because both men prophesied to gentile nations.

From their safe dwellings, the gentile nation of Edom gloated over Israel's destruction. Because of this attitude, God sent Obadiah to prophesy that Edom would be destroyed—and it was. This one short prophecy is all we know about Obadiah.

God sent Jonah to prophesy to the town of Nineveh, today known as Mosul in northern Iraq, but he ran away. He knew God was merciful, that people would repent, and his prophecy would not come true. When Jonah obeyed and preached to Nineveh, that is exactly what happened.

Some may wonder if Jonah's story is true. Jesus verified the story by comparing His burial to Jonah's experience:

> For as Jonah was three days and three nights in the belly of a huge fish, so the Son of Man will be three days and three nights in the heart of the earth. (Matthew 12:40)

Prophetic books help us understand God. Though He is sovereign over all nations, He still hears the cry of individuals in difficult circumstances.

> From inside the fish Jonah prayed to the LORD his God. He said: "In my distress I called to the LORD, and he answered me." (Jonah 2:1-2)

Prayer: Lord, when we feel as desperate as Jonah, help us know that You hear us when we cry out to You.

He has shown you,
O mortal, what is good.
And what does
the LORD require of you?
*To act justly and
to love mercy and
to walk humbly
with your God.*

Micah 6:8

What Does the Lord Require of You?

*S*ometimes we think of prophets as musicians playing in a minor key. Because prophets carry warnings of judgment, we think that is their only message. But prophets also include messages of hope.

Micah carried both messages. He lived when kings ruled, before Judah went into the Babylonian captivity. He prophesied to both nations, warning of coming judgment for their sins.

When people asked what God wanted, Micah called for justice and right living—much like Amos had a few years earlier. He said:

> He has shown you, O mortal, what is good.
> And what does the LORD require of you?
>
> To act justly and to love mercy,
> and to walk humbly with your God. (6:8)

In this statement, Micah sums up the Old Testament law. Jesus replied similarly when He said the greatest commandments were to love God and to love others as ourselves.

Micah included other clear prophecies—that the Messiah would be born in Bethlehem and that Israel would one day be restored. He ends his prophecy with a message of hope:

> Who is a God like you,
> who pardons sin and forgives the transgression
> of the remnant of his inheritance?
> You do not stay angry forever
> but delight to show mercy. (7:18)

Prayer: Lord, help us live in right relationship with You and others using the guidelines You and Micah give us.

The LORD is good,
a refuge in times of trouble.
He cares for those who trust in him.

Nahum 1:7

A Good and Just God

*H*ow do you picture God when you pray? Nahum portrays God as good but also just. His justice requires judgment, which we don't like to think about.

Nahum predicts coming judgment on Nineveh because of its sin. When Jonah preached to Nineveh in the previous century, the city repented and God withheld judgment. That doesn't happen this time.

Nahum describes God as jealous, avenging, and wrathful. Immediately he clarifies the description, saying God expresses wrath slowly and only on the unrepentant.

Nahum goes on to say God will bring judgment to the powerful city of Nineveh and keep the little nation of Judah secure. His prophecies seemed improbable then, but from our vantage point of history, we know he was right.

Why is this account included in the Bible? Does it matter what happened to Nineveh almost 3,000 years ago? By reading it, we see God's involvement in history and know He is also involved today.

Our history is still being written, but God has not changed. Nahum's portrayal of God is still true. He says,

> The LORD is good,
>   a refuge in times of trouble.
> He cares for those who trust in him,
>   but with an overwhelming flood . . .
> he will pursue his foes into the realm of darkness. (1:7-8)

Prayer: Lord, help us remember that You are good, but You are also just. We trust You to act according to who You are.

The just *shall live*
by his faith.

Habakkuk 2:4, KJV

God Is in Control

*W*hen I read Habakkuk, I chuckle because I understand his feelings about God exactly. I just haven't expressed my questions so honestly.

We know little about Habakkuk, a contemporary of Jeremiah, who lived when the nation of Israel crumbled. Habakkuk doesn't think God is listening or doing anything about the wickedness around him.

Attempts to communicate with God seem useless. Then God tells Habakkuk not to worry; He is sending the Chaldeans to capture Israel.

Shocked, Habakkuk reminds God—as if He didn't know—that the Chaldeans are worse than the Israelites. Then Habakkuk sets himself on a tower to watch what God will do.

God teaches Habakkuk a valuable lesson—to look beyond his circumstances to see the big picture. Wickedness was all around, but that would not always be so.

God introduced to Habakkuk a principle that both the apostle Paul and Martin Luther picked up much later, familiarly expressed as, "The just shall live by his faith" (2:4, KJV).

God reminds Habakkuk of His authoritative position:

> The LORD is in his holy temple:
> let all the earth be silent before him. (2:20)

Habakkuk was silenced by this declaration. His powerful prayer in the next chapter shows him moving from doubt to faith. In spite of conflicting circumstances, he could trust God and rejoice in Him by faith.

Prayer: Lord, help us learn faith as Habakkuk did, to remember that You are in control, even when it does not seem You are.

The Lord your God
is with you,
The Mighty Warrior
who saves.
He will take
great delight
in you;
in his love
he will no longer
rebuke you, but
will rejoice
over you
with singing.

Zephaniah 3:17

God Is Present, Powerful, and Purposeful

*W*e meet a variety of people when we read the prophets. Besides the cartoon type and the anonymous ones, we've met a shepherd, priests, and statesmen. Now we meet a member of the royal family.

Zephaniah lists his connection with kings for some reason. For us, it shows the scope of God's concern. He cares for all segments of society.

Zephaniah prophesied before the fall of Jerusalem; his themes are similar to those of other prophets: God will bring judgment for the sins of Israel. Zephaniah also portrays a clear picture of the heart of God.

> The LORD your God is with you,
>> the Mighty Warrior who saves.
>
> He will take great delight in you;
>> in his love he will no longer rebuke you,
>> but will rejoice over you with singing. (3:17)

An analysis of this verse shows that God is present, God is powerful and God is purposeful—three characteristics of God to keep in focus as we communicate with Him.

But the verse also shows a side of God's personality we don't often think about. God is pleased with His people—so much so that He sings!

God does not rejoice in bringing judgment to the ungodly, but He does rejoice when He sees people doing what is right.

Prayer: Lord, I want everything in my life to cause You to sing!

"But now be strong . . . ,"
declares the Lord,
"Be strong . . . and work.
For I am with you."

Haggai 2:4

Covenant-Making God

"Don't get the cart before the horse" was another generation's way of saying: "Put first things first." Haggai's prophecy says the same thing.

Haggai appears without introduction. He directs his four prophecies to Zerubbabel, the man who led the Jews back to their homeland, ending the Babylonian captivity. People busy themselves building homes while neglecting the temple. Then they wonder why God is not blessing them.

Haggai exhorts the people to "put first things first" to experience God's blessing. Jesus taught a similar lesson:

> But seek first his kingdom and his righteousness, and all these things will be given to you as well. (Matthew 6:33)

At first, the people respond positively, but they soon become negligent. Again, Haggai prophesies, reminding them of God's promise:

> "But now be strong . . .," declares the LORD. "Be strong . . . and work. For I am with you." (2:4)

God reminds them that He is the covenant-making God who brought them out of Egypt, and He is still with them.

When the prophecies continue, they are about the coming Messiah, causing the hearers to look to the future when God will "shake the nations" and "what is desired by all nations" will come (2:7). Haggai encourages them to remember the past, to look beyond the present, and see God's plan for the future.

Prayer: Lord, help us to grasp what Haggai teaches; help us to live now in the light of eternity.

The Lord will be king
over the whole earth.
On that day
there will be one Lᴏʀᴅ
and his name the only name.

Zechariah 14:9

Knowing the Future

*W*hen a novel gets intense, do you turn to the end of the book to see how it turns out? That's what prophets do for us. They give us glimpses of the future to help us cope with the present.

Zechariah follows the same themes as his contemporary, Haggai. Both were concerned with the present but prophesied of the future.

We quote many of Zechariah's prophecies about the Messiah. Among other things, he foretold:

- The ride into Jerusalem on a donkey (9:9).
- The betrayal for 30 pieces of silver (11:12).
- The Crucifixion (13:7, also quoted by Jesus in Mark 14:27).

Zechariah foretold the Messiah's first coming, which assures us that his prophecies about the Messiah's ultimate reign will also be fulfilled.

> On that day his feet will stand on the Mount of Olives, east of Jerusalem. (14:4)

> The LORD will be king over the whole earth. On that day there will be one LORD, and his name the only name. (14:9)

Zechariah's prophecies were intended as encouragement to the people who were living in seemingly hopeless conditions, that a better day was coming. That is why we read him today, to know the future is not as hopeless as the present sometimes seems.

Prayer: Lord, help us see Your kingdom as clearly as Zechariah did, for our hope is in You, not in any political system.

Then those
who feared the Lord
talked with
each another, and
the Lord listened
and heard.

Malachi 3:16

God Offers Hope

*C*ommunication with God is not always prayerful. Malachi records an argument between God and His people.

We know little about Malachi. His writings indicate he lived in the period of restoration, possibly a contemporary with Nehemiah.

The argument begins when God tells Israel of His love. They respond by asking: "How have you loved us?" God reminds them He blessed Israel but judged unrepentant Edom (1:1-4).

God questions their love:

> If I am a father, where is the honor due me? If I am a master, where is the respect due me? (1:6)

They question God's justice so He challenges them:

> You have wearied the LORD with your words . . . . By saying, "All who do evil are good in the eyes of the LORD, and he is pleased with them," or "Where is the God of justice?" (2:17)

God questions their sincerity by their failure to bring offerings:

> Will a mere mortal rob God? Yet you rob me. But you ask, "How are we robbing You?" In tithes and offerings. (3:8)

In spite of this, God offers hope:

> Then those who feared the LORD talked with each other, and the LORD listened and heard. A scroll of remembrance was written. (3:16)

God overhears private conversations. He remembers those who remember Him.

Prayer: Lord, forgive us when we question You; count us with those who sincerely fear You and honor Your Name.

For the law was given
through Moses;
grace and truth came
through Jesus Christ.

John 1:17

The "Silent Years"

*D*id God speak in the years between the Old and New Testaments? Sometimes those are called "silent years." No prophetic voice is recorded, but history continued to be written as the prophets predicted.

Daniel's vision of four political powers (Daniel 2:19-43) became a reality. Judah passed from the Babylonians, to the Persians, to the Greeks, and finally to the Romans. Romans are in power during the New Testament period.

Many Jewish traditions changed during the intertestamental period. For example, the sacred writings were translated from Hebrew into the Greek language in the Septuagint.

God may not have been speaking directly, but He was definitely working, preparing for one of the greatest events in human history. When the timing was right, He sent His Son. Galatians 4:4 declares, "But when the set time had fully come, God sent his Son, born of a woman, born under the law."

That sentence gives us a simple fact, but the centuries reveal the significance of Christ's birth. John summed it up in one verse:

> For the law was given through Moses; grace and truth came through Jesus Christ. (John 1:17)

Christ was born under the Law, but His birth brought grace. The entire New Testament helps us understand what that means.

Prayer: Lord, thank You for sending Your Son; help us appreciate all that His coming means—and live accordingly.

Therefore
go and make disciples
of all nations,
baptizing them
in the name of the Father
and of the Son
and of the Holy Spirit,
and teaching them
to obey everything
I have commanded you.

Matthew 28:18-20

Sharing the Gospel

*H*ave you observed the similarities between the Old and New Testaments? The Old Testament starts with Genesis, the Book of Beginnings. The New Testament introduces a new beginning, signaled by the birth of Christ.

The Old Testament begins with the Law, Israel's foundation. The New Testament begins with the Gospels, the Church's foundation. Righteousness in the Old Testament comes by obedience to the Law. New Testament righteousness comes by faith in Christ; obedience follows.

The Gospel writers address various cultural groups, giving different perspectives of Christ's ministry. John says they didn't tell it all because the world couldn't hold that many books (John 21:25).

Matthew, a former tax collector, traces Jesus' genealogy to Abraham. His book links the themes of the Old Testament to the New Testament.

Matthew 6:9–13 gives "The Lord's Prayer," a model for communicating with God. Jesus directs us to approach God as "Father," then He continues with the elements of prayer:

Worship	"Hallowed be Your Name"
Intercession	"Your kingdom come"
Petition	"Give us today"
Repentance	"Forgive us"
Guidance	"Lead us"

Older translations include a conclusion:

Submission	"For thine is the kingdom"

Matthew doesn't limit his message to Jews but charges all his readers to carry the good news to the entire world (28:18-20).

Prayer: Lord, help us remember Matthew's teaching about prayer and sharing the gospel with the world.

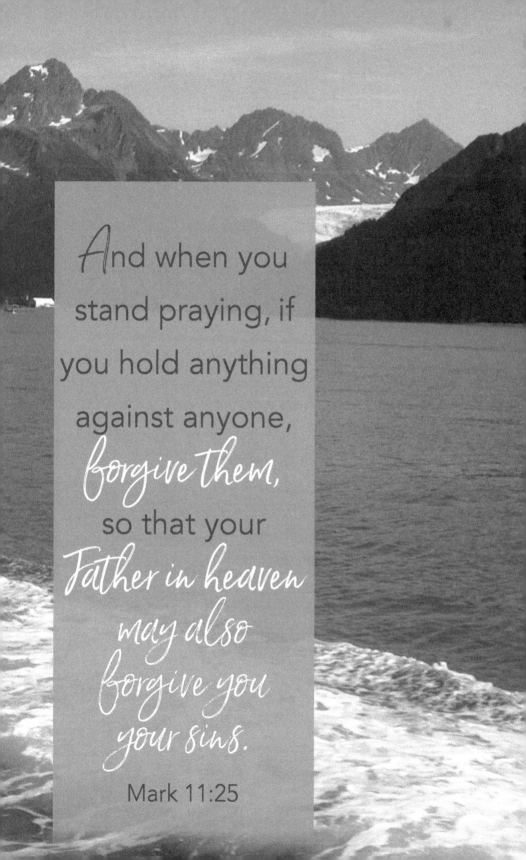

And when you stand praying, if you hold anything against anyone, *forgive them,* so that your *Father in heaven may also forgive you your sins.*

Mark 11:25

A Second Chance

*R*eading Mark should encourage anyone who "blows it" early in life. Mark is the poster boy for success when given a second chance.

In the Book of Acts we meet Mark as a young man at his mother's home. He accompanies Paul on his first journey but soon deserts him. Paul refuses to take Mark again. Later their relationship is restored.

Early church writings say Mark traveled with Peter in ministry. Mark's knowledge of Christ's life probably came from Peter. His writing style suggests he was writing to the Greco-Roman world. We have Mark's writing because believers gave him a second chance.

Mark records Jesus' teaching on prayer after His triumphal entry into Jerusalem. On the way, Jesus denounces a barren fig tree. The next morning, the disciples note the fig tree is withered. Jesus then gives a teaching on prayer. He begins: "Have faith in God" (Mark 11:22).

He follows that statement by emphasizing two elements faith must include: believing for results and forgiving others.

> Truly I tell you, if anyone says to this mountain, "Go, throw yourself into the sea," and does not doubt in their heart but believes that what they say will happen, it will be done for them. Therefore I tell you, whatever you ask for in prayer, believe that you have received it, and it will be yours. And when you stand praying, if you hold anything against anyone, forgive them, so that your Father in heaven may forgive you your sins. (11:23–25)

Prayer: Lord, give us faith to believe and to receive and grace to forgive others because we need Your forgiveness.

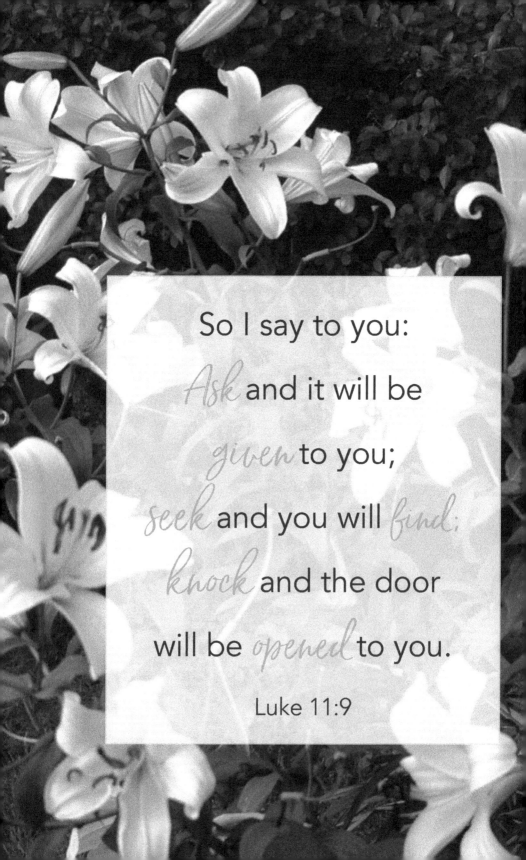

So I say to you:
Ask and it will be
given to you;
seek and you will *find*;
knock and the door
will be *opened* to you.

Luke 11:9

Prayer in Action

*L*uke could be a TV reporter today. In his introduction, he says he has investigated the facts about Jesus and talked to eyewitnesses about His ministry. His Gospel begins very much like the evening news.

Likewise, the gospel accounts are as varied as evening news reports. Matthew, a Jew, gives the insider's report, emphasizing the Jewish point of view. Mark focuses on action more than teaching, seemingly to appeal to non-Jewish readers.

Luke, a Greek physician, gives the investigative report and eyewitness interviews. He pursues truth as a basis for faith. Luke's writings are for all believers, though he addresses his account to Theophilus, an unknown individual, whose name means "lover of God."

Luke emphasizes the humanity of Jesus and the universality of His ministry. His themes are summed up in one verse:

> For the Son of Man came to seek and to save the lost. (19:10)

His teaching on prayer includes descriptions of Jesus praying before important events. Luke emphasizes the teaching on the Lord's Prayer by adding the importance of persistence in prayer:

> So I say to you: Ask and it will be given to you; seek and you will find; knock and the door will be opened to you. (11:9)

Prayer is more than verbalization of desire; it includes earnestness, and sometimes, action in accordance with our request.

Prayer: *Lord, we long to communicate with You; teach us how to pray earnestly, and prompt us when we need action with our prayers.*

For God so loved
the world
that he gave
his one and
only Son,
that whoever
believes in him
shall not perish
but have
eternal life.

John 3:16

Believing in Jesus

Who was Jesus' closest friend on earth? His siblings did not believe He was the Messiah until after the Resurrection.

Early in ministry, Jesus calls two brothers, James and John. Along with Peter, they become His closest companions. On the cross, Jesus assigns His mother to John. John, the first disciple at the tomb, immediately believed in the resurrection.

From being close to Jesus, John knows His heart. He writes primarily about Jesus' last week. He understands why Jesus came and emphasizes it in his writing:

> But these are written that you may believe that Jesus is the Messiah, the Son of God, and that by believing you may have life in his name. (20:31)

Believing in Christ is emphasized throughout John's Gospel. A well-known verse states this theme clearly:

> For God so loved the world that he gave his one and only Son, that whoever believes in him shall not perish but have eternal life. (3:16)

This verse summarizes the Bible. We see God's purpose, His power, and His love. We see His compassion for humanity, for whom He gave His Son. Those doomed to eternal death are offered eternal life by believing in Christ.

In an open invitation, God's love offers transforming hope to all who by faith believe in Jesus and accept His offer of salvation.

Prayer: Lord, we affirm our faith in You, and we receive Your salvation. Thank You for giving Your life for us; we give our lives to You.

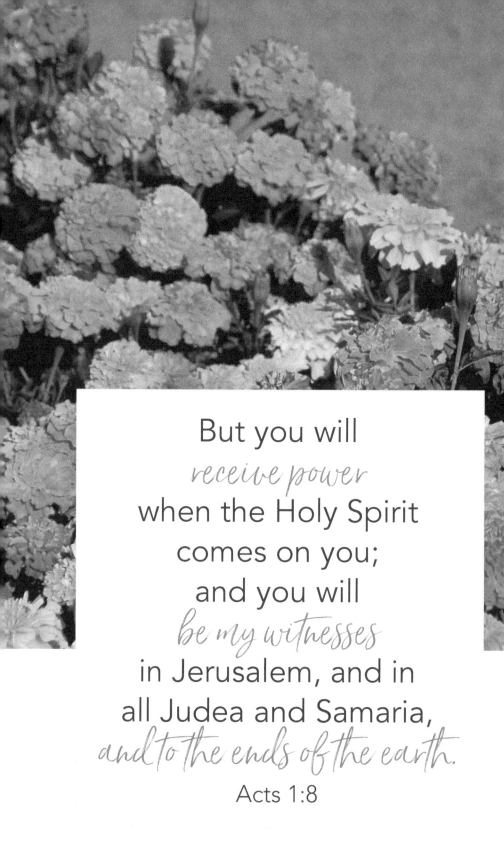

But you will
receive power
when the Holy Spirit
comes on you;
and you will
be my witnesses
in Jerusalem, and in
all Judea and Samaria,
and to the ends of the earth.
Acts 1:8

The Holy Spirit Comes

*H*istory is recorded after it happens. We have only one historical book in the New Testament because the Church was just beginning.

Twelve historical books follow the Old Testament Law. Only one historical book, The Acts of the Apostles, follows the Gospels in the New Testament

The Gospels offer little detail about Jesus' ascension. In Acts 1, Luke, the author of the Book of Acts, records that event and Jesus' last words:

> But you will receive power when the Holy Spirit comes on you; and you will be my witnesses in Jerusalem, and in all Judea and Samaria, and to the ends of the earth. (1:8)

This verse summarizes the Book of Acts where we read of the coming of the Holy Spirit. We learn how the Spirit leads believers from Jerusalem to Samaria and into the gentile world.

Some have said the book could be named the Acts of the Holy Spirit, because the disciples moved in the Spirit's power.

In Acts 2, Peter concludes his dynamic sermon:

> Repent and be baptized, every one of you, in the name of Jesus Christ for the forgiveness of your sins. And you will receive the gift of the Holy Spirit. The promise is for you and your children and for all who are far off—for all whom the Lord our God will call. (2:38–39)

The Church is still empowered by the Holy Spirit today.

Prayer: Lord, we desire Your presence in our lives; cleanse us from sin and fill us with Your Spirit.

I am not ashamed
of the gospel,
because it is
the power of God
that brings
salvation
to everyone
who believes.

Romans 1:16

Righteousness by Faith

*B*efore the Internet, getting mail in the mailbox was a daily highlight. Before modern postal systems were developed, couriers took months to deliver letters personally.

Much early Christian teaching was communicated by courier letters, preserved in the Bible as the Epistles. In the Old Testament, Writings follow the Historical section; likewise in the New Testament, the Epistles follow the Gospels and the Book of Acts.

The Book of Romans introduces the writings of Paul, a Jew who persecuted Christians before he converted to Christianity. The Book of Acts records his conversion and ministry. Most of the Epistles are his writings—his letters to congregations he helped form. Paul was educated in Judaism and understood its relationship to Christianity.

Romans is a book directed to the church in Rome that probably was started by the "strangers from Rome," listed in Acts 2 on the Day of Pentecost. As in most epistles, Paul deals with doctrinal issues and then teaches Christian living.

Early in Romans, Paul teaches that right standing with God comes only through faith in Jesus Christ, not by doing good works.

> For I am not ashamed of the gospel, because it is the power of God that brings salvation to everyone who believes . . . . For in the gospel the righteousness of God is revealed—a righteousness that is by faith . . . just as it is written: "The righteous will live by faith." (1:16-17)

He quotes Habakkuk that faith puts us in right relationship with God. Our works show our love for God.

Prayer: Lord, help us understand our righteousness in Christ; then, help us live righteously by loving others.

And now these three remain:
faith, hope and love.
But the greatest of these
is *love.*

1 Corinthians 13:13

The Greatest Is Love

Do you remember the first time you heard the gospel? You may have heard Christian teaching all your life. The Corinthian people were not so blessed.

Corinth, a thriving metropolis at the crossroads of trade routes, had many temples to pagan gods. Immorality was rampant.

To this debauchery, Paul brought the message of God's love. The Corinthians depended on his teaching, but his only means of communication was letters by couriers.

First and Second Corinthians are two of those letters in which Paul teaches a different way of life. In the first letter, Paul discusses their position in Christ and their call to be holy (1:2).

He deals with problems of immorality and idolatry. He teaches appropriate worship and manifestation of spiritual gifts. He teaches about the resurrection of the dead and eternal life.

Just as Jesus summed up the Law as loving God and others, Paul gives his well-known teaching on the supremacy of love as a "better way" of life:

> And now these three remain: faith, hope and love. But the greatest of these is love. (1 Corinthians 13:13)

The Apostle Paul's second letter to the Corinthians was a defense of his own ministry and the teachings about Christ he knew to be true. His conclusion will be our conclusion today:

> May the grace of the Lord Jesus Christ, and the love of God, and the fellowship of the Holy Spirit be with you all. (2 Corinthians 13:14)

Prayer: *Lord, we pray with Paul for the grace and love of God to be with all of our friends.*

But the fruit of the Spirit
is love, joy, peace,
forbearance, kindness, goodness,
faithfulness, gentleness
and self-control.

Galatians 5:22-23

The Fruit of the Spirit

*H*ow do you tell when a watermelon is ripe? On my grandfather's farm we thumped melons and listened for the sound. In the Book of Galatians, the Apostle Paul gives some clues for the sounds of mature spiritual life.

Early in Paul's letter to the Galatians, we read what we saw in Habakkuk and Romans—that salvation is by faith:

> Know that a person is not justified by the works of the law, but by faith in Jesus Christ. (2:16)

Our faith in Jesus puts us in right standing with God.

Paul also teaches that faith produces righteous living, evidenced by the fruit of the Spirit in our lives. In Chapter 5, he is very specific about life practices produced by the sinful nature.

Likewise, Paul is very specific about ways the Spirit works in our lives:

> But the fruit of the Spirit is love, joy, peace, forbearance, kindness, goodness, faithfulness, gentleness and self-control. (5:22-23)

I think of these qualities as keys to good relationships in different areas of my life. My relationship with God is characterized by love, joy, and peace. My relationship with others needs mutual tolerance (forbearance), kindness, and goodness. As for myself, I need integrity (faithfulness), gentleness, and self-control.

This teaching sounds like Jesus' teaching in the Gospels that the sum of the Law is loving God and loving our neighbor as ourselves.

Prayer: Lord, thank You for giving Your Spirit to help us live this life of love in all relationships.

And *pray in the Spirit*
on all occasions with all kinds
of prayers and requests.
With this in mind,
be alert and always keep on praying
for all the LORD's people.

Ephesians 6:18

Spiritual Armor

*B*eing dressed for the occasion sometimes means more than making a fashion statement. Athletes, metalworkers, and mountain climbers are among those who dress appropriately for their activities.

In writing the Book of Ephesians, Paul gives instructions for being appropriately dressed for spiritual warfare.

Ephesians differs from other epistles in that Paul does not address any specific church problems. The masterfully written epistle is divided evenly between spiritual teaching and instructions for living.

Paul concludes by describing a well-dressed Christian soldier. An analysis of the attire sounds like a summarization of Paul's teaching.

For spiritual warfare, the believer clothes himself with truth and righteousness. His mind trusts securely in his salvation; his faith serves as a shield from doubt. His weapons—the Word and the Spirit of God—"are not the weapons of the world. On the contrary, they have divine power to demolish strongholds" (2 Corinthians 10:4).

A military man always carries orders. The marching orders for this soldier are:

> And pray in the Spirit on all occasions with all kinds of prayers and requests. With this in mind, be alert and always keep on praying for all the Lord's people. (Ephesians 6:18)

Spiritual battles are won by spiritual methods. The believer, well dressed in spiritual armor, knows prayer is the greatest means of winning spiritual victories.

Prayer: Lord, help us to be appropriately dressed and equipped to fight our daily spiritual battles.

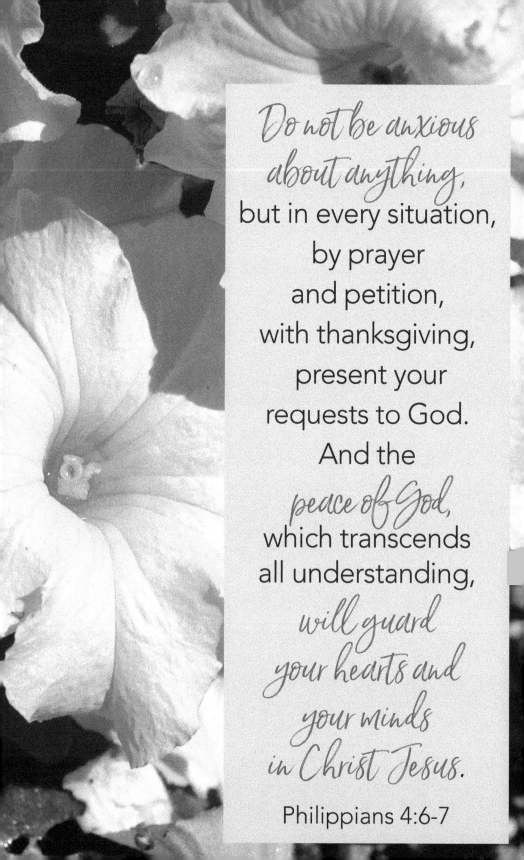

Do not be anxious about anything, but in every situation, by prayer and petition, with thanksgiving, present your requests to God. And the *peace of God*, which transcends all understanding, *will guard your hearts and your minds in Christ Jesus.*

Philippians 4:6-7

Prayer and Peace

*C*lose friendships often form among people who go through harrowing experiences together. The Philippians reading this letter would remember Paul's experience in their city.

Paul wrote this letter from Rome while a prisoner there; he had also been in prison in Philippi. According to Acts 16, Paul and Silas were worshiping the Lord at midnight when an earthquake loosened their prison chains. The jailer and his household accepted the Lord after this miracle. This epistle is written to friends Paul made in Philippi.

The opening statement in Philippians reveals Paul's consistent prayer life. He tells the Philippians that he prays for them; He prays,

> That your love may abound yet more and more in knowledge and depth of insight; so that you may be able to discern what is best and may be pure and blameless. (1:9-10)

In summary, he prayed they would have abounding love, make good choices, and live good lives—a good pattern for our prayers.

As he closes, he encourages prayer as an alternative to worrying:

> Do not be anxious about anything, but in every situation, by prayer and petition, with thanksgiving, present your requests to God. And the peace of God, which transcends all understanding, will guard your hearts and your minds in Christ Jesus. (4:6-7)

The pattern here is to continue prayer, petition, and thanksgiving until they have peace, a pattern we would do well to follow.

Prayer: Lord, help us bring our anxieties to You, to pray until we have peace.

And *whatever* you do,
whether in *word or deed*, do it all
in the name of the Lord Jesus.

Colossians 3:17

Staying in Tune with God

*H*ave you heard an orchestra tune up before a symphony? It sounds discordant, but they are all tuning to the key of "A." Getting that first note right is essential.

The Colossians were slightly "off-pitch" doctrinally. Paul helped tune their thinking to center on Christ, their beginning note. Paul uses lavish language portraying Christ's supremacy:

> He is before all things, and in him all things hold together. And he is the head of the body, the church; he is the beginning and the firstborn from among the dead, so that in everything he might have the supremacy. (1:17-18)

When Paul is certain they picture Christ correctly, he summarizes:

> And whatever you do, whether in word or deed, do it all in the name of the Lord Jesus. (3:17)

Paul's final challenge to them is to maintain communication with God:

> Devote yourselves to prayer, being watchful and thankful. (4:2)

Though not in biblical order, we include the Book of Philemon here because it was possibly sent with the letter to the Colossians.

Paul writes a note to Philemon regarding Onesimus, Philemon's runaway slave, converted in prison with Paul. The letter requests Philemon to live "in tune" with Paul's instructions to the Colossians by welcoming Onesimus as a brother in Christ rather than as a runaway slave. Our relationship to Christ should be reflected in our relationship to others.

Prayer: Lord, help us to see You clearly, to make You the center of our lives, so we live in tune with Your purposes.

Make it your ambition
to lead a *quiet life* . . .
so that your *daily life*
may win the
respect of outsiders.

1 Thessalonians 4:11-12

Living in the Present

Farmers plant crops in straight rows by keeping their eyes looking straight ahead. Only occasionally do they look down around them.

Paul gave similar advice to the Thessalonians, a church suffering intense persecution. He reminds them to keep their eyes on the Lord's coming while enduring the present circumstances.

Every chapter in 1 Thessalonians refers to the Lord's coming. Second Thessalonians carries the same theme.

After Jesus' ascension, the angels said He would return just as He went away (Acts 1:11). Early believers thought He would come in their lifetime. Some had died and believers were confused. Paul assures them their loved ones will live again:

> For the Lord himself will come down from heaven . . . and the dead in Christ will rise first. After that, we who are still alive . . . will be caught up together with them. . . . And so we will be with the Lord forever. (1 Thessalonians 4:16,17)

Paul wants the Thessalonians to look for Christ's return and live circumspectly in the present. He tells them to

> Make it your ambition to lead a quiet life . . . so that your daily life may win the respect of outsiders." (4:11-12)

Prayer: Lord, help us to live like the farmers plowed crops, with eyes on the future but fully aware of the present.

All Scripture is God-breathed and is useful for teaching, rebuking, correcting and training in righteousness.

2 Timothy 3:16

Passing the Faith On

All value systems are just one generation from extinction; values continue only when they are passed to the next generation.

Jesus told His followers to preach and make disciples. The word *disciples* really just means "students" or "learners." Paul charged Timothy and Titus to continue his work after he was gone.

First Timothy and Titus are similar letters, written after Paul was released from his first imprisonment. Both carry instructions for continuation of his work.

Like a father speaking to sons, Paul gives his "sons in the Gospel" instructions on church organization and relationships. He tells them how to conduct their personal lives as ministers of the Gospel.

Second Timothy, written from Paul's final imprisonment, has a different tone. When time is short, an old man focuses on what is most important.

The propagation of the message of Jesus was Paul's highest priority. He wanted Timothy to continue his work:

> Do your best to present yourself to God as one approved, a worker who does not need to be ashamed and who correctly handles the word of truth. (2 Timothy 2:15)

He repeatedly emphasizes the importance of God's Word:

> All Scripture is God-breathed and is useful for teaching, rebuking, correcting and training in righteousness. (2 Timothy 3:16)

Paul wrote these words while chained in a dungeon. He wisely believed God's Word was worth living for and worth dying for.

Prayer: Lord, help us to treasure Your Word as Paul did, and to share it with the next generation.

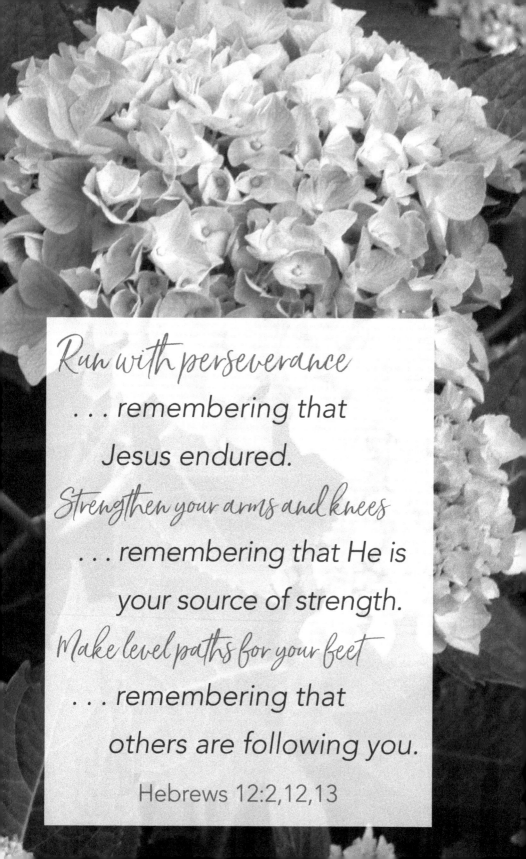

Run with perseverance
. . . remembering that
Jesus endured.
Strengthen your arms and knees
. . . remembering that He is
your source of strength.
Make level paths for your feet
. . . remembering that
others are following you.

Hebrews 12:2,12,13

Run with Strength

*T*he anonymous writer of Hebrews sounds like Paul talking to the Thessalonians, when he says "Fixing our eyes on Jesus" (12:2). The first ten chapters of Hebrews tell us why he says that. Repeatedly, the writer shows us how Jesus excels.

As the Son of God, Jesus is higher than angels who are created beings. As a Son, He is better than Moses who was a chosen servant. As a priest, He is better than Aaron because He ministers eternally in heaven.

Christ's priesthood presides over an eternal covenant. The old law was written on stone; His law is written in the hearts of those who fear God. Old covenant sacrifices were offered repeatedly; Christ's sacrifice was made once for all.

In Hebrews 12, the writer exhorts new believers to fix their "eyes on Jesus," the foundation for their faith. He uses the metaphor of a runner to teach how believers should live the life of faith.

"Run with perseverance" (12:2)
. . . *remembering that Jesus endured.*

"Strengthen your . . . arms and weak knees" (12:12)
. . . *remembering that He is your source of strength.*

"Make level paths for your feet" (12:13)
. . . *remembering that others are following you.*

Other practical instructions follow, concluding with a prayer for God to equip them for every good work.

Prayer: Lord, help us remember who You really are. We need Your help to run the race faithfully.

If any of you lacks wisdom, you should ask God, who gives generously to all without finding fault, and it will be given to you.

James 1:5

Living Our Beliefs

*W*ho said that? Knowing who is talking helps us understand what the message is. This knowledge is helpful when reading the Book of James.

The author of James is not the disciple who was Jesus' close friend that became one of the first martyrs. This James was Jesus' half-brother, the oldest son of Joseph and Mary (Matthew 13:55). He was also martyred for his beliefs.

This James did not follow Jesus until after the Resurrection. He was not present at the Crucifixion; otherwise, Jesus would not have asked John to care for Mary, His mother. Jesus appeared to James after the Resurrection. James was with the disciples in the Upper Room.

However, James does not claim his sibling relationship with Jesus. He introduces himself as "James, a servant of God and of the Lord Jesus Christ" (1:1). He uses the word for a voluntary servant, not a slave.

James speaks authoritatively, sounding very much like an older brother. He directs us to God in our quest for wisdom, encouraging us to ask in faith and we will receive:

> If any of you lacks wisdom, you should ask God, who gives generously to all without finding fault, and it will be given to you. (1:5)

James emphasizes living our beliefs; a basic premise is "faith without deeds is dead" (2:26). He encourages prayer in faith, believing God for answers:

> The prayer of a righteous person is powerful and effective (5:16).

Prayer: Lord, help us live our faith as James teaches; may our prayers be powerful and effective.

But *grow in the grace,*
and knowledge
of our Lord and Savior

Jesus Christ.

2 Peter 3:18

Growing in Grace

*H*ave you ever lived in a foreign country? If so, you know that hearing from home satisfies like a drink of water when you are thirsty.

Peter's letters would have been like that to Christians scattered throughout the Roman world. He reminds them of their position in Christ and how their faith affects their life.

"Grace and peace be yours" are some of Peter's opening words. Then he talks about living in grace.

Jews followed the Law of Moses that told them how to live; Romans had pagan gods that shaped their lives. Without similar guidelines, how were believers in Christ supposed to live in grace?

Peter says grace gives hope in Christ because of forgiven sins, a hope appropriated by faith, not works. This hope, made alive by faith, produces love—fervent love for God and for other people as ourselves. Living in grace means living in love, because of our faith and hope.

Peter says love is expressed by respect in relationships and personal self-control. If submission to authority brings suffering, we follow Christ's example for suffering. Peter keeps before his readers the hope of eternal life with Christ.

Second Peter is a reminder that Christian maturity is a process:

> But grow in the grace and knowledge of our Lord and Savior Jesus Christ. (2 Peter 3:18)

Prayer: Lord, this world sometimes seems foreign to us; help us know how to live in grace and love.

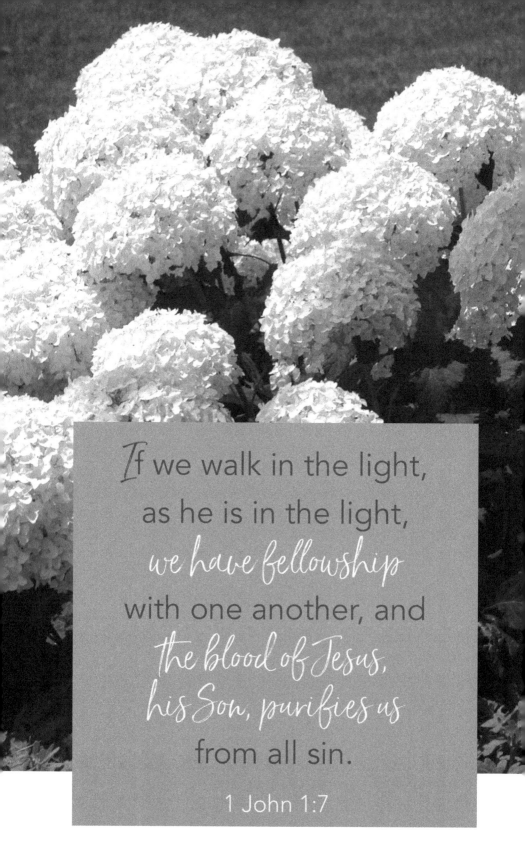

If we walk in the light,
as he is in the light,
we have fellowship
with one another, and
the blood of Jesus,
his Son, purifies us
from all sin.

1 John 1:7

Walking in Light

*D*oes loving God mean "anything goes"? Or does love have boundaries?

John identifies himself as the "disciple whom Jesus loved" several times in his writings. He writes about God's love, but also emphasizes truth. For John, love in truth definitely sets boundaries.

The Early Church was dealing with false teaching about the deity of Jesus. John's opening statements reaffirm Jesus' deity when he says Jesus "was with the Father and has appeared to us" (1 John 1:2).

Using the metaphor of light, John explains how believers should live in Christ:

> If we walk in the light, as he is in the light, we have fellowship with one another, and the blood of Jesus, his Son, purifies us from all sin. (1 John 1:7)

All three letters of John continue this premise.

In the first epistle, John says walking in light is walking in truth. Repeatedly in his epistles, John refers to truth. For John, truth matters!

Walking in truth means receiving cleansing from sin through the death of Christ. Because Christ was truly the Son of God, His death effectively cleanses from sin.

Walking in truth produces right relationship with God and others. John summarizes God's laws as Jesus did. Love for God overflows in love for others. Love for God respects truth as revealed in His Word.

Prayer: Lord, may truth be enlivened in our lives; help us live in loving relationship with You and others.

Building yourselves up in your most holy faith and praying in the Holy Spirit, keep yourselves in God's love . . .

Jude 1:20-21

Living in Love

*D*oes it matter what we believe, as long as we are sincere? Jude, like John, says a resounding: "Yes!" New Testament writers were so sure of their beliefs that many of the writers died for them.

Jude, brother of Jesus, came to faith after the Resurrection. He felt so strongly that truth matters that he left writing about doctrine to write a corrective epistle. He says, "I felt compelled to write and urge you to contend for the faith" (1:3).

Jude's reason was that erroneous teaching had been presented, similar to what John had corrected in his epistles. The teaching denied Christ's deity and permitted people to live immoral lives.

Jude reminds believers that in the Old Testament, God judged unrepentant sinners, regardless of who they were. Even angels were judged if they abandoned God's purposes.

He concludes with a call to believers to be aware of false teaching. They should avoid error that appeals to natural desires and denies God's authority over mankind.

His conclusion gives basic guidelines for Christian living:

> But you . . . building yourselves up in your most holy faith and praying in the Holy Spirit, keep yourselves in God's love . . . (1:20-21)

Jude reiterates principles taught by John and other disciples.

Prayer: Lord, You are so faithful in giving Your Word. Help us be as faithful in living by it.

Blessed
is the one
who reads aloud
the words of
this prophecy.

Revelation 1:3

The Gift of Eternal Life

*I*s heaven real or just a fantasy? Jesus talked about His heavenly home. He assured His followers He was preparing a place for them as well (John 14:1-2).

Many New Testament writers refer to the blessed hope of eternity with the Lord. Revelation, the only prophetic book in the New Testament, tells more about it.

John the apostle, while imprisoned on the island of Patmos, received visions of heaven. The symbolic language is challenging, but John says:

> Blessed is the one who reads aloud the words of this prophecy. (1:3)

When John saw the glorified Jesus in his vision, he was awestruck and "fell at his feet as though dead" (1:17). Jesus assured John He was the same person John had known as a close friend before.

Jesus instructed John to "Write, what you have seen, what is now and what will take place later" (1:19). Revelation follows that outline. Chapters 1 to 3 give what John has seen and is seeing; other chapters tell what happens later.

We hear about God's throne and streets of gold. These are described in the last chapters. The book closes with words of blessing to the one who "keeps the words of the prophecy" (22:7).

Revelation ends with an open invitation:

> Let the one who is thirsty come; and let the one who wishes take the free gift of the water of life. (22:17)

Prayer: Lord, thank You for the invitation to spend eternity with You. By faith we accept that free gift of eternal life.

For Further Reading

This book is designed as an introduction to reading through the Bible annually. I hope it will encourage many readers in this practice. Establishing a regular time and place for Bible reading is a good beginning.

Establishing a consistent method of reading is the second step. The traditional method used for many years was three chapters each weekday and four chapters on Sunday to get through the Bible in the year.

Bibles are available specifically designed for daily readings for the year. As technology has advanced, annual Bible readings also are available online.

Continual effort is the final step, accompanied with determination to develop the habit of annual Bible reading. Achieving the goal will be worth the effort.

Notes

Notes

To purchase more copies of

Gathering Wisdom

A Devotional Walk through the Books of the Bible

visit **http://www.xulonpress.com/bookstore/**
or
Amazon.com.

To find the author on Facebook, search for:
Monday Meditations—by Peggy Musgrove.

CPSIA information can be obtained
at www.ICGtesting.com
Printed in the USA
LVHW02s2358201017
553069LV00004B/6/P